Hard-to-See Animals

WITHDRAWN

By Allan Fowler

Consultants

Linda Cornwell, Learning Resource Consultant,
Indiana Department of Education

Fay Robinson, Child Development Specialist

Children's Press®
A Division of Grolier Publishing
New York   London   Hong Kong   Sydney
Danbury, Connecticut

Project Editor: Downing Publishing Services
Designer: Herman Adler Design Group
Photo Researcher: Caroline Anderson

Library of Congress Cataloging-in-Publication Data

Fowler, Allan.
    Hard-to-see animals / by Allan Fowler.
      p. cm. – (Rookie read-about science)
    Includes index.
    Summary: Illustrations and brief text describe how different animals use their
coloring to blend into their surroundings.
    ISBN 0-516-20548-X (lib. bdg.) 0516-26259-9 (pbk.)
    1. Color of animals—Juvenile literature. [1. Color of animals.
2. Camouflage (Biology)] I. Title. II. Series
QL767.F68   1997   96–46955
591.47'2—dc21   CIP
                                  AC

       7 8 9 10 R 06 05 04 03 02 01

What do you see in this picture?

If you didn't see much of anything, look again. Look for a moth. Now can you find it?

The moth is the same color as the tree bark it's resting on.

If you didn't notice the moth the first time you looked . . . neither would an animal that eats moths.

An animal has less chance
of being eaten if it is the
same color as the things
around it.

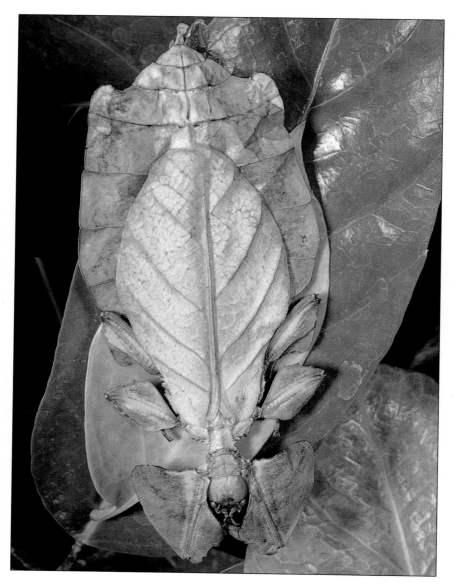

6

A green insect on a leaf
is hard for a hungry frog
to see.

This one is even shaped
like a leaf.

If it doesn't move, it could
be mistaken for a leaf.

This white hare is hard
for a wolf to see against
white snow.

And in the spring, when the snow melts, the hare will still be hard to see because its fur then turns light brown.

Some flatfish are the same color as the sea bottom.

Can you see the fish here?

These fish have bright
colors and bold patterns.
You might think they
would be very easy to see.

But they live among coral
reefs, which have varied
colors and shapes. Against
a coral reef, the fish do not
stand out.

Stripes or spots or patchy colors can help an animal blend in with its surroundings.

Imagine how strongly these zebras would stand out against trees or bushes if they were all white or all black.

Being hard to see also helps an animal that attacks other animals. The whiteness of a polar bear . . .

the stripes on a tiger . . .

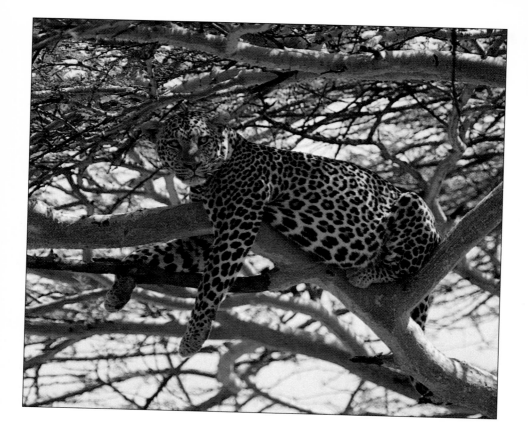

or the spots on a leopard . . .
enable it to get closer to its
prey before being seen.

18

Some animals can change their color to match their surroundings. Lizards called chameleons do it very quickly.

This flap-necked chameleon
changed its color to look
like its background.

An octopus not only changes color, it also hides from its enemies by squirting a swirl of black ink from its body.

lionfish

Certain fish, like sea
dragons and lionfish,
are covered with spines.

sea dragon

They look like part
of the plant life where
they swim.

A hermit crab might hide by covering its borrowed shell with sea anemones or seaweed.

When people want to hide, they may use some of the same tricks as animals.

A soldier who wears a uniform with patches of green and brown, or who covers his helmet with leaves or twigs, is hard for an enemy to see.

This is called camouflage.

Do you think that people got the idea for camouflage from some of the animals you've just seen?

Or *not* seen?

Words You Know

chameleon

insect

moth

camouflage

hare

leopard

polar bear

tiger

zebras

coral reef

lionfish

sea dragon

octopus

Index

About the Author

Allan Fowler is a free-lance writer with a background in advertising.
Born in New York, he lives in Chicago now and enjoys traveling.

Photo Credits

©: Animals Animals: 11 (G.I. Bernard), 6, 20, 30 top right, 30 top left (E.R. Degginger), 22, 31 bottom left (Laurence Gould), 16, 31 top right (Breck P. Kent), 19, 21, 31 bottom right (Zig Leszczynski), 27, 30 bottom right (C.C. Lockwood), 29 (J.H. Robinson), 17, 31 middle left (Anup Sham), 9, 31 top left (Stouffer Productions Ltd.); Norbert Wu Photography: 12, 13, 23, 31 bottom center, 31 middle right; Photo Researchers: 3, 30 bottom left (Scott Camazine), 8 (Alan D. Carey), cover (Stephen Dalton) 15, 31 center (Gregory G. Dimijian), 24 (Fred McConnaughey), 5 (M. H. Sharp), 18, 31 top center (Peter Skinner).